Sodium

and the Alkali Metals

THE PERIODIC TABLE

Nigel Saunders

www.heinemann.co.uk/library
Visit our website to find out more information about Heinemann Library books.

To order:
 Phone 44 (0) 1865 888066
 Send a fax to 44 (0) 1865 314091
Visit the Heinemann Bookshop at www.heinemann.co.uk/library to browse our
catalogue and order online.

First published in Great Britain by Heinemann Library, Halley Court, Jordan Hill, Oxford OX2 8EJ, part of Harcourt Education.
Heinemann is a registered trademark of Harcourt Education Ltd.

Editorial: Dr Carol Usher and Sarah Eason
Design: Ian Winton
Illustrations: Stefan Chabluk
Picture Research: Vashti Gwynn
Production: Edward Moore

Originated by Ambassador Litho Ltd
Printed and bound in Hong Kong, China by South China Printing Company

ISBN 0 431 16994 2
08 07 06 05 04
10 9 8 7 6 5 4 3 2 1

British Library Cataloguing in Publication Data
Saunders, N.(Nigel)
Sodium and the alkali metals.
- (The periodic table)
546.3 ' 8

A full catalogue record for this book is available from the British Library.

Acknowledgements
The publishers would like to thank the following for permission to reproduce photographs:
Corbis pp8 (Dex Images), **10**, **11** (L Clarke), **15** (Ron Watts), **29** (Paul A. Souders), p**31** (Roger Ressmeyer), **32** (Science Picture Limited), **35** (George Shelley, Inc.) **40** (Buddy Mays), **41** (Doug Wilson), **45** (Adam Hart-Davis), **47** (Tom Stewart), **49** (Neal Preston), **55** (CRDPHOTO); Discovery Books Picture Library pp**1**, **22**, **23**, **33**; Hotpoint p**25**; Science Photo library pp**9** (Francoise Sauze), **12**, **13** (Jerry Mason), **17** (Charles D Winters), **20** (Sheila Terry), **27** (R Maisonneuve, Publiphoto Diffusion), **28** (Martyn F Chillmaid), **36** (John Greim), **58** (James L Amos, Peter Arnold Inc.), **42** (Sinclair Stammers), **45** (Adam Hart-Davis), **46** (Quest), **50**, **52** (Alexandra Tsiaris), **54** (Chris Priest), **56** (American Institute of Physics), **57** (Fermilab).

Cover photograph of salt crystals reproduced with permission of Corbis.

The author would like to thank Angela, Kathryn, David and Jean for all their help and support.

Every effort has been made to contact copyright holders of any material reproduced in this book. Any omissions will be rectified in subsequent printings if notice is given to the publishers.

Disclaimer
All the Internet addresses (URLs) given in this book were valid at the time of going to press. However, due to the dynamic nature of the Internet, some addresses may have changed, or sites may have ceased to exist since publication. While the author and publishers regret any inconvenience this may cause readers, no responsibility for any such changes can be accepted by either author or the publishers.

Contents

Words appearing in bold, **like this**, are explained in the Glossary

Elements and atomic structure

There are millions of different substances around us. Some of them are gases, such as air; others are liquids, such as water; but most of them are solids, as is this book. They do have one thing in common however: they are all made from just a few simple substances called **elements**.

▲

Everything you can see here, including the train, cars and buildings, is made from some of the millions of substances in the world. Some of the substances, for instance the oxygen in the air, will be elements, but most will be compounds.

Elements and compounds

Elements are substances that cannot be broken down into anything simpler by using chemical **reactions**. There are about ninety elements that occur naturally and scientists have learned how to make over twenty more using **nuclear reactions**. Approximately three-quarters of the elements are metals, such as sodium, the rest are non-metals, such as chlorine. Elements can join together in countless different ways in chemical reactions to make **compounds**. An example of this is when sodium and chlorine react together to make the compound sodium chloride, which is table salt. Most of the millions of different substances in the world are compounds, made up of two or more elements chemically **bonded** together.

Atoms

Every substance, whether it is an element or a compound, is made up of tiny particles called **atoms**. An element contains just one type of atom whereas compounds are made from two or more different types of atom joined together. Although we can see most of the substances around us, individual atoms are far too tiny for us to see, even with a light microscope. Francium atoms are the biggest of the **alkali** metals but even if you could stack a million of them on top of each other, the pile would only be about half a millimetre high!

Subatomic particles

Scientists used to think that atoms were the smallest things in the universe. However, they now know that atoms are made from even smaller objects called **subatomic particles**. The biggest ones, called **protons** and **neutrons**, are joined together in the centre of the atom to form a **nucleus**. Smaller subatomic particles, called '**electrons**', are arranged in layers, or 'shells', around the nucleus. This arrangement of electrons resembles the way the planets are arranged around the Sun. Most of an atom is actually empty space!

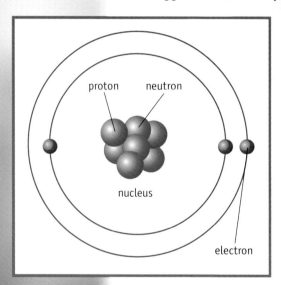

◀ *This is a model of a lithium atom. Each lithium atom contains three protons and four neutrons, with three electrons arranged in two shells or energy levels around the nucleus.*

Groups

Chemistry is exciting and unpredictable because the elements all react in different ways. Several attempts were made to sort the elements to make things more predictable, but it was a Russian chemist called Dimitri Mendeleev who was the most successful. In 1869 he made a table where each element was placed into one of eight **groups**, with similar elements in each group. This made it much easier for chemists to work out what to expect. Mendeleev's table was so successful that the modern **periodic table** developed from it.

The periodic table, sodium and the alkali metals

The modern **periodic table** shown here is based closely on Mendeleev's table. The **elements** are arranged in horizontal rows called **periods**, with the **atomic number** (number of **protons** in the **nucleus**) increasing from left to right. Each vertical column in the periodic table is called a **group** and the elements in each group have similar chemical properties. There are eighteen groups altogether.

Elements in a group all have the same number of **electrons** in the shell furthest from the **nucleus**, called the outer shell. For example, the elements in group 2 are all metals with two electrons in their outer shells, whereas the elements in group 7 are non-metals with seven electrons in their outer shells. The elements in both groups **react** quickly with other substances. The periodic table gets its name because the elements are arranged so that their different chemical properties occur regularly or periodically.

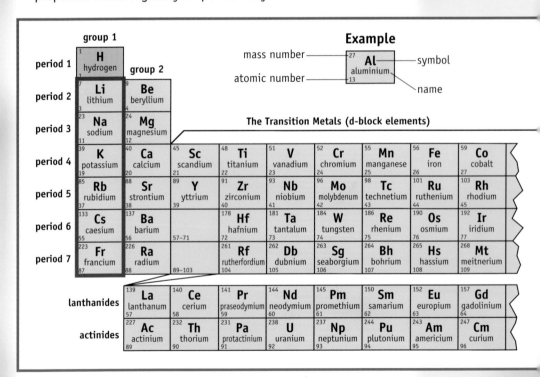

The properties of the elements change gradually as you go down a group, for example in group 0 the elements become **denser**. Balloons filled with helium (at the top of the group) rise quickly into the air, which is why they are such fun at parties. Balloons filled with argon (from the middle of the group) fall slowly. However, balloons filled with xenon from the bottom of the group fall to the ground very quickly indeed.

Sodium and the alkali metals

The elements in group 1 are all metals. They are often called the **alkali** metals because they produce alkalis when they react with water. They are usually too soft and reactive for anything to be built out of them, but their **compounds** are extremely useful to us in many ways. In this book you will find out all about sodium, the other alkali metals and many of their uses.

▼ *This is the periodic table of the elements. Group 1 contains lithium, sodium, potassium, rubidium, caesium and francium, which are all metals.*

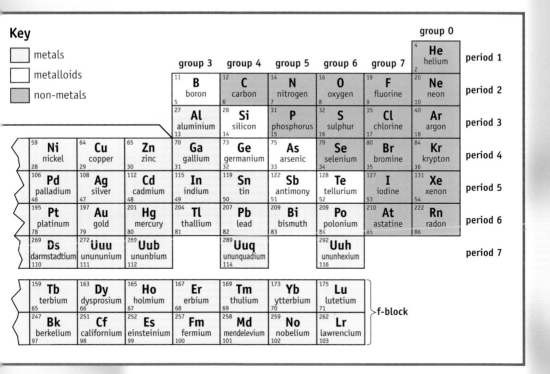

Introducing the elements of group 1

There are six **elements** in **group** 1, lithium, sodium, potassium, rubidium, caesium and francium (as you descend the group). They are fairly soft, silvery-white metals and all **react** with water to make **alkaline** solutions. They are all solids at room temperature, but the melting points of rubidium and caesium are low enough for them to become liquids on very hot days.

7 **Li** lithium 3	**lithium** *symbol: Li • atomic number: 3 • metal*

What does it look like? Lithium is soft enough to be cut fairly easily with a steel knife. At first the cut surface is shiny but quickly becomes dull because the exposed metal reacts with oxygen in the air to form lithium oxide. This is why pieces of lithium often look grey. Lithium is usually stored in oil to stop the element reacting with water and oxygen in the air.

Where is it found? Lithium is too reactive to be found naturally as a pure metal. Instead, it is found all over the world as various **compounds** in **minerals** such as spodumene and lepidolite.

What are its main uses? Lithium is mixed with other metals to make **alloys** used by the aircraft industry and to make batteries for laptop computers. Lithium compounds have many uses, including cosmetics, heat-resistant cookware and devices, called scrubbers, that keep the air supply safe for astronauts to breathe.

Batteries containing lithium are used in many electronic devices, including watches, mobile phones and laptop computers. ▶

23
Na
sodium
11

sodium

symbol: Na • atomic number: 11 • metal

What does it look like?   Just like lithium, sodium can be cut easily with a knife, revealing a shiny surface. This reacts with oxygen in the air to form a dull layer of sodium oxide in seconds, making it appear light grey. Sodium is normally stored in oil to block any reactions with water and oxygen in the air.

Where is it found?   Sodium is the sixth most abundant element in the Earth's crust and it is found, as a compound, in many minerals including borax (sodium borate) and Chile saltpetre (sodium nitrate). The most common sodium mineral is rock salt (sodium chloride). The oceans contain vast quantities of sodium chloride, which is the main compound that makes the sea salty.

▼ *These salt pans in France produce 3000 tonnes of salt (sodium chloride) a year. The salt is left behind as water evaporates from the shallow pools of seawater.*

What are its main uses?   Sodium is used in nuclear power stations and to **extract** titanium metal. Sodium chloride is used as table salt and to make many other compounds, which are important for the manufacture of many familiar things including glass, paper, plastics and detergents.

More elements of group 1

39	
K	
potassium	
19	

potassium
symbol: K • atomic number: 19 • metal

What does it look like?   Pieces of potassium often look dark grey, even though the metal is silvery, because they are covered by potassium oxide. Potassium is soft enough to be moulded using finger pressure. To prevent it **reacting** with air and water, it is usually stored in oil.

Where is it found?   Potassium is the eighth most abundant **element** in the Earth's crust, but because it is so reactive it is only found as a **compound**. It is present in many **minerals** including potash (potassium hydroxide), and sylvite (potassium chloride). The sea also contains a lot of potassium compounds.

What are its main uses?   Potassium compounds are widely used in **fertilizers** to help crops grow properly and in explosives for fireworks and mining.

85	
Rb	
rubidium	
37	

rubidium
symbol: Rb • atomic number: 37 • metal

What does it look like?   Rubidium is a very soft, silvery metal. In a very hot climate, rubidium may become a liquid as it melts at only 39 °C. It is usually stored in a very unreactive gas such as argon because rubidium would react with just about everything else.

Where is it found?   Rubidium is not found naturally as a pure metal because of its reactivity. Several minerals contain tiny amounts of rubidium compounds, but it is much rarer than lithium, sodium or potassium. Rubidium is usually obtained from the waste material produced when lithium is **extracted** from lepidolite.

What are its main uses?   Rubidium is used in photoelectric cells and in electronic devices called vacuum tubes.

133 Cs caesium 55	**caesium**
	symbol: Cs • atomic number: 55 • metal

What does it look like?   Caesium (pronounced 'see-zee-um') is a very soft metal with a very faint gold colour. It is very reactive and must be stored in a **vacuum** or an unreactive gas such as argon. Caesium melts at 28 °C and would become a liquid if you held its container.

Where is it found?   The metallic form of caesium is not found naturally and it is even rarer than rubidium. A mineral called pollucite contains caesium aluminium silicate, but caesium is usually extracted from the materials left over when lithium is obtained from lepidolite.

What are its main uses?   Caesium is used in atomic clocks, which are incredibly accurate and keep clocks all over the world in step with each other. **Radioactive** caesium is used to treat cancer.

◀ *Potassium nitrate is an ingredient of gunpowder, which is used in spectacular fireworks like these.*

223 Fr francium 87	**francium**
	symbol: Fr • atomic number: 87 • metal

What does it look like?   Francium is very radioactive, and nobody has actually seen enough of it for us to know what it looks like. However, chemists expect it to be a very soft, silvery metal – just like the other **alkali** metals.

Where is it found?   Francium is incredibly rare. There are probably only a few grams of it in the whole of the Earth's crust at any one time! If scientists want to study francium, they make it using **nuclear reactions**.

What are its main uses?   Francium has no commercial uses, but research scientists study it to see if their predictions about its properties are accurate.

Trends in group 1

The **alkali** metals **react** with oxygen, water and dilute acid in similar ways. However, the reactions are not identical because the metals become more reactive going down the **group** (as the **atomic number** increases). A gradual change in a property like reactivity is called a trend. Lithium at the top of the group is the least reactive, potassium near the middle is more reactive than lithium, and francium at the bottom is the most reactive. Unfortunately, it is almost impossible to study the chemistry of francium because it is **radioactive** and very rare.

Reactions with acids

All the alkali metals react with acids to produce metal salts and hydrogen gas, H_2. The salt formed depends upon the metal and acid used. For example, if sodium reacts with hydrochloric acid, HCl, it makes sodium chloride, NaCl.

> *The word equation for the reaction of sodium with hydrochloric acid is:*
>
> sodium + hydrochloric acid $\rightarrow$ sodium chloride + hydrogen
>
> $$2Na + 2HCl \rightarrow 2NaCl + H_2$$

If sodium reacts with sulphuric acid, H_2SO_4, it makes sodium sulphate, Na_2SO_4.

> *The word equation for the reaction of sodium with sulphuric acid is:*
>
> sodium + sulphuric acid $\rightarrow$ sodium sulphate + hydrogen
>
> $$2Na + H_2SO_4 \rightarrow Na_2SO_4 + H_2$$

Reactions with oxygen

All the alkali metals react with oxygen to form metal oxides. For example, sodium reacts with oxygen to produce sodium oxide, Na_2O, and potassium reacts with oxygen to produce potassium oxide, K_2O.

This is molten sodium metal burning in oxygen. The reaction between sodium and oxygen is very vigorous, producing a bright flame and clouds of white sodium oxide. ▶

When lithium is heated in air, it ignites with a small white flame, while sodium burns with an orange flame. If burning lithium or sodium is lowered into a jar of pure oxygen gas, they both burn more brightly and produce clouds of lithium oxide or sodium oxide, which are both white.

The word equation for the reaction of sodium with oxygen is:

sodium + oxygen → sodium oxide

*This sort of reaction is called a synthesis reaction because a **compound** is made by chemically combining its **elements**.*

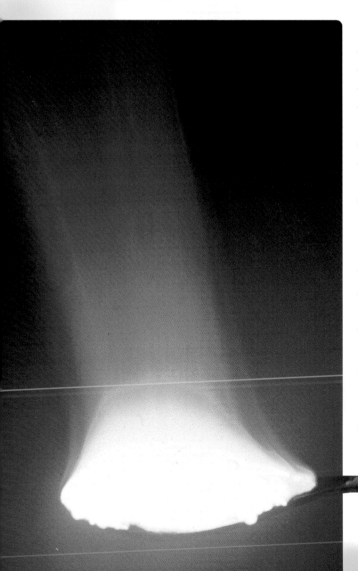

Potassium burns in air with a lilac-coloured flame. When lowered into a jar of pure oxygen the potassium burns more quickly and the flame becomes so hot that it turns white, producing clouds of white potassium oxide, K_2O. Rubidium and caesium are even more reactive than potassium. They ignite and react with the oxygen in the air without being heated first. Rubidium produces brown rubidium superoxide, RbO_2, and caesium produces orange-red caesium superoxide, CsO_2.

Colourful chemistry

Each salt of the **alkali** metals produces its own characteristic colour when it is put into a flame. If some table salt is sprinkled into a Bunsen burner flame, the sodium in the salt turns the flame bright orange. The flame colour depends upon the metal in the salt and chemists can use these 'flame tests' to work out which metal is in an unknown salt.

Flame tests

A loop of platinum wire is used in flame tests. For a good result it must be really clean, so it is immersed into concentrated nitric acid and rinsed in distilled water. The loop is then dipped into the salt or its solution and held in the hottest part of the Bunsen burner flame. The flame changes colour depending upon the metal in the salt.

Excited, but not for long

When energy such as heat is applied to an **atom** its **electrons** become excited and jump into a shell further from the **nucleus**. Electrons cannot stay in this 'excited' state for long and they fall back to a shell closer to the nucleus, letting go of their extra energy as light. Big falls produce blue light and small falls red light. Each element forms a unique **spectrum** of colours because its electrons make different jumps and falls.

▼ *Electrons can jump into another shell if they are given the right amount of energy. When they fall back to their normal shell, they give out this energy as light.*

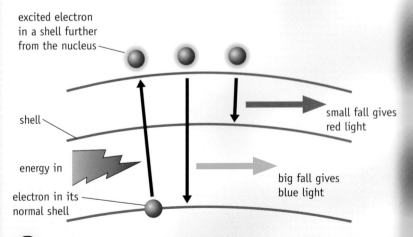

excited electron in a shell further from the nucleus

shell

energy in

electron in its normal shell

small fall gives red light

big fall gives blue light

All the colours of the rainbow

White light has a spectrum that is made up of all the colours. These are red, orange, yellow, green, blue, indigo and violet. **Prisms** split light up so that its spectrum is displayed. A device called a **spectroscope** is used to study the light given out during a flame test. Simple spectroscopes contain a prism to split the light into its spectrum. Gustav Kirchhoff was the first person to realize that every element produces a different spectrum.

Two German scientists, Gustav Kirchhoff and Robert Bunsen, used a spectroscope to study the light emitted in flame tests. They discovered caesium in 1860 and rubidium in 1861 as a result. A new type of burner provided the very hot flame needed for their experiments. Although called the Bunsen burner, it was actually designed and built by Peter Desaga, a technician at the University of Heidelberg where Bunsen worked.

Street lamps

Heat is not the only form of energy that can cause atoms to emit light. Gases trapped inside tubes at below normal pressure will glow if electricity is passed through them. Fluorescent lights and neon lights work like this. Sodium street lamps produce orange light because electricity is passed through sodium vapour. Neon gas is used to start up these lamps so they make a red glow when they are first switched on. As the lamp warms up, sodium metal is vaporized and the light turns orange.

▲
Sodium lamps produce more light for the same amount of electrical energy than many ordinary light bulbs. They are often used to light streets and motorways at night.

Reactions with water

All the **alkali** metals **react** with water to produce a metal hydroxide and hydrogen gas. For example, sodium reacts with water to produce sodium hydroxide, NaOH.

The word equation for sodium reacting with water is:

sodium + water → sodium hydroxide + hydrogen

The metal hydroxides are white solids that dissolve easily in water, making the water alkaline. However, the reactions become more dangerous going down the group from lithium to caesium.

Lithium

When lithium is dropped into water it fizzes and floats on the surface. It gradually becomes smaller until it eventually disappears. The lithium does not vanish; it reacts with the water to produce soluble lithium hydroxide. Universal indicator, which is a mixture of dyes used to tell if a substance is acidic, alkaline or neutral, turns purple when added to the water, showing that the lithium hydroxide solution is alkaline. The fizzing is caused by the hydrogen gas made in the reaction. This can be set alight and although it should burn with a colourless flame, it has a red colour because some lithium **atoms** are present.

Sodium

So much heat is produced by the reaction when sodium is dropped into water that it melts into a shiny ball. This whizzes around, producing lots of bubbles of hydrogen gas and leaving a trail of white sodium hydroxide. Eventually it disappears with a small popping sound. The sodium hydroxide dissolves into the water making it alkaline. If a few drops of water are dropped on to a piece of sodium, the heat builds up until the sodium catches fire with an orange flame and lots of smoke.

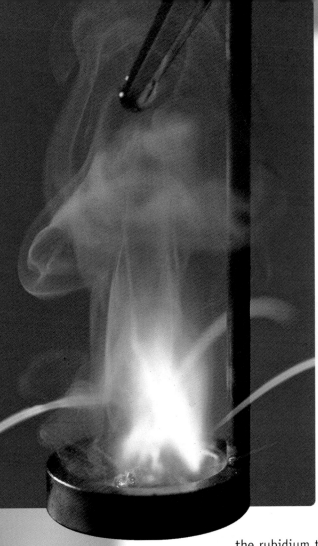

This is potassium reacting with drops of water to make potassium hydroxide and hydrogen gas. The hydrogen burns with a flame coloured lilac by vaporized potassium.

Potassium

The reaction between potassium and water is very fast. When water is dripped on to potassium, the potassium ignites straight away with a lilac flame and sparks. If a small piece of potassium is added to water, it floats and immediately catches fire. The metal disappears within a few seconds and the reaction produces potassium hydroxide and hydrogen gas.

Rubidium

Rubidium and water react extremely fast. As soon as the rubidium touches the surface of the water it explodes in a shower of sparks and red flames, producing rubidium hydroxide and hydrogen. Molten pieces of rubidium may shoot out of the water. You are unlikely to see your teacher demonstrate this reaction because it is so dangerous.

Caesium and francium

When caesium reacts with water it is incredibly hazardous. After being dropped into water caesium sinks, producing lots of hydrogen bubbles as it goes. It then explodes very violently, producing caesium hydroxide and hydrogen. Caesium is so reactive it even reacts with ice at -100 °C! As francium is extremely rare, it is unlikely that anyone has ever investigated how it reacts with water, but chemists expect it to be even more dangerous than caesium.

What causes the reactivity trend?

The **electrons** in an **atom** are arranged in shells around its **nucleus**. The outer shell is the furthest from the nucleus and the most important one for chemists. In most cases this is completely full when it contains eight electrons. Atoms with full outer shells are very stable and unreactive, and include helium, neon and the other noble gases in **group** 0.

The outer shells of the other **elements** are not completely filled with electrons. These atoms react with others to fill them up. In a chemical **reaction** between a metal like sodium and a non-metal such as chlorine, the atoms fill their outer shells by passing electrons from one to the other. The **compound** formed, sodium chloride, is stable and unreactive.

Electrons hold the key

Metal atoms have unfilled outer shells often containing only one, two or three electrons. They give these electrons to other atoms during chemical reactions and the full shell underneath becomes their new outer shell. In contrast, non-metal atoms have outer shells with usually just one, two or three electrons short of being full. It is simpler for non-metal atoms to receive electrons from other atoms to complete their outer shells.

The **alkali** metals have atoms with only one electron in their outer shell. During a reaction with non-metals, these single electrons are transferred to the non-metal atoms. The easier it is to transfer the electron, the more reactive the alkali metal.

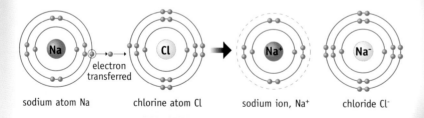

sodium atom Na   chlorine atom Cl   sodium ion, Na⁺   chloride Cl⁻

▲
*When sodium reacts with chlorine, each sodium atom transfers its outer electron to a chlorine atom. This produces electrically-charged particles called **ions**, which are attracted to each other and form strong chemical bonds.*

Transfer those electrons

Lithium atoms are the smallest in group 1 and not very reactive. The electron in the outer shell is close to the nucleus of the atom and is very strongly attracted to it. This makes the transfer of an electron to a non-metal atom relatively difficult. Moving down group 1, the atoms become larger and correspondingly more reactive. As the distance between the electron and the nucleus increases the attraction between them lessens and it is easier for the electron to be transferred during reactions. Francium, at the bottom of the group, has the largest atoms and should be the most reactive. However, its rarity and **radioactivity** make it difficult to study.

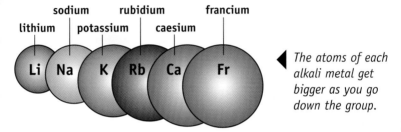

The atoms of each alkali metal get bigger as you go down the group.

The reactivity series

If metals are listed in order of their reactivity, with the most reactive metal first, the list is called a reactivity series. Chemists can make a really big reactivity series by studying the reactions of other metals, not just the alkali metals. By looking at a metal's position in the series they can predict how it should react.

element		group
potassium	most reactive	1
sodium		1
lithium		1
calcium		2
magnesium		2
aluminium		3
zinc		transitional metal
iron		transitional metal
tin		4
lead		4
copper		transitional metal
silver		transitional metal
gold		transitional metal
platinum	least reactive	transitional metal

Lithium

Lithium is a soft silvery metal that **reacts** quickly with air and water. Storing it in oil stops this happening.

The discovery of lithium

Johan Arfwedson, a Swedish chemist, discovered lithium in 1817. Arfwedson was studying a **mineral** called petalite to search for potassium **compounds**, but the compounds he **extracted** from the petalite had different properties from those he expected. He was sure that he had discovered a new **element**, which he named lithium from the Greek word for stone. Unfortunately he was only able to isolate some lithium compounds, not the metal itself. A year later, an English chemist called Sir Humphry Davy, used a process called **electrolysis** to isolate lithium metal.

Sir Humphry Davy isolated lithium metal using electricity in 1818. He also discovered sodium and potassium in 1807 and became the first person to isolate magnesium, calcium, strontium and barium, in 1808.

Lithium minerals

Lithium is rare in the Earth's crust, on average each tonne of rock only contains about twenty grams of it. However there are several minerals that contain lithium compounds in large enough amounts to make them worth mining. These include petalite, spodumene, lepidolite and amblygonite, which are all complex compounds. Chile is the biggest single producer of lithium **ores**, but China and Australia are also major producers. Around forty thousand tonnes of lithium are used in the world each year, mostly as lithium compounds rather than the metal itself.

Extracting lithium

Several steps are needed to extract lithium from its ores. The ore is crushed, heated strongly and then mixed with sulphuric acid. A solution of lithium sulphate is produced and filtered to remove impurities. Sodium carbonate is added to the filtered lithium sulphate solution and solid lithium carbonate is formed. The lithium carbonate is dried, then sold to chemical companies so that they can produce other lithium compounds.

Lithium metal is produced from lithium chloride by electrolysis. The lithium chloride is melted and electricity passed through it. Lithium is formed at the negative electrode and chlorine gas is produced at the positive electrode.

Electrolysis

Electrolysis is a process that chemists use to split compounds into simpler substances, usually the elements they contain. The compound is first melted or dissolved in water and then an electric current is passed through it between two 'electrodes'. These are metal or graphite rods that conduct electricity and they are dipped into the compound. Usually, metals form at the negative electrode and non-metals form at the positive electrode. During the electrolysis of molten lithium oxide, lithium forms at the negative electrode and oxygen at the positive electrode. Sir Humphry Davy used this method to isolate lithium, sodium and many other metals from their compounds.

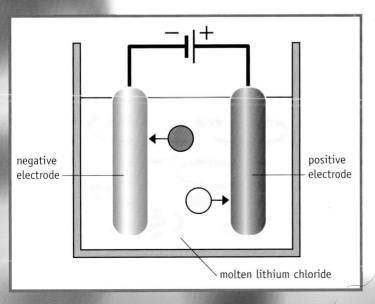

negative electrode

positive electrode

molten lithium chloride

*During electrolysis of molten lithium chloride, positively-charged lithium **ions** are attracted to the negative electrode and become lithium **atoms**. Chloride ions are attracted to the positive electrode and form chlorine gas.*

Uses of lithium

Lithium is a more **reactive** metal than many others are, so it is useful for removing unwanted substances, such as oxygen, from brass and copper. Although lithium is too reactive and soft to be used on its own to build things, it can be mixed with other metals to produce **alloys** with very useful properties.

Lithium in space

Aluminium is a metal with a low **density**, which means that objects made from it are light for their size. The large external fuel tank on the space shuttle was originally made from an aluminium alloy that contained six per cent copper to give it increased strength. An aluminium alloy containing one per cent lithium and four per cent copper is now used to make the external fuel tank.

The Space Shuttle Discovery lifting off from the Kennedy Space Center in Florida, USA. The large brown-coloured fuel tank is made from a strong, but lightweight, aluminium-copper-lithium alloy. Each fuel tank contains two and a half tonnes of lithium.

These new tanks are over three tonnes lighter than the original tanks and allow the space shuttle to ferry heavier objects into space. Each tank contains around two and a half tonnes of lithium. They are the only part of the space shuttle that cannot be reused – they fall back to Earth when they are empty and burn up in the atmosphere.

Lithium batteries

Many modern electronic devices need batteries that are lightweight and produce a lot of electricity for their size. Lithium is a very useful metal for batteries because it has a low density and is therefore light. It is also a very reactive metal, so it can provide a high voltage.

Electricity and the reactivity series

A simple battery can be made by dipping two different metals into a beaker of weak acid or salty water. Electricity will flow through a wire if it is connected to the dry ends of the metals. The further apart the two metals are in the reactivity series, the bigger the voltage. A battery made from zinc and copper develops 1.1 volts (V), but one made from lithium and copper could develop as much as three times that. Battery designers work hard to design batteries that produce a useful current and are long-lasting.

The negative electrode in a lithium battery is made from lithium or lithium-aluminium alloy. Lithium batteries develop about 3V, twice the voltage of ordinary batteries and produce electricity for a longer time. Lithium batteries come in a wide variety of sizes, including tiny button batteries used in watches, calculators and electronic car keys. Larger lithium batteries are used in radios, cameras and as back-up power supplies for computer memory chips.

Lithium carbonate

Some people suffer from an illness called manic depression or bipolar disorder. This means that they have severe mood swings, sometimes being very happy and confident, but at other times becoming very miserable. Lithium carbonate tablets are the most successful medicine for reducing these symptoms. Lithium carbonate is very important in industry as well, about forty-five thousand tonnes of it are used each year. Although lithium is often mixed with aluminium to form **alloys**, lithium carbonate has an important role to play in the **extraction** of aluminium from bauxite, its **ore**.

Aluminium production

Aluminium is extracted from bauxite using **electrolysis**. The bauxite is treated to produce aluminium oxide, which is then melted. When electricity is passed through the molten aluminium oxide, it breaks down to form aluminium at the negative electrode and oxygen at the positive electrode. Unfortunately, a lot of energy is needed to melt the aluminium oxide because it has a high melting point. A **mineral** called cryolite is used to reduce its melting point, saving energy and making aluminium cheaper to produce. If lithium carbonate is also added, the melting point of aluminium oxide is reduced even more. This is one of the most common uses for lithium in industry, but it is not the only one.

Cryolite

Aluminium oxide needs to be molten to produce aluminium using electrolysis, but will only melt at over 2000 °C. However aluminium oxide dissolves in cryolite, Na_3AlF_6, a mineral that melts at just over 1000 °C. Like lithium carbonate, this reduces the energy needed to produce molten aluminium oxide, saving a lot of money.

Making glass

Glass is made when sand is melted then cooled very quickly. However, sand melts at over 1700 °C! To reduce the melting temperature to about 800 °C sodium carbonate is usually added, but lithium carbonate is often added too. Another advantage of adding lithium carbonate, Li_2CO_3, is that it breaks down in the heat to form lithium oxide, Li_2O, and carbon dioxide, CO_2. Glass containing lithium oxide is stronger than ordinary glass and does not expand as much when it is warmed up. It is used to make heat-resistant glassware for kitchens and laboratories.

▼ *Glass ceramics contain lithium compounds and are used for making missile nose cones, ovenware and ceramic cooker hobs because they are hardly affected by changes in temperature.*

Lithium carbonate is different

*Lithium carbonate is the only **alkali** metal carbonate that will decompose or break down when heated. If you tried to decompose sodium carbonate by heating, not much would happen – it would just get very hot! However, if you heat lithium carbonate, lithium oxide and carbon dioxide are formed:*

$$\text{lithium carbonate} \xrightarrow{\text{heat}} \text{lithium oxide + carbon dioxide}$$

More lithium compounds

The chemical industry uses complex lithium **compounds** as **catalysts** for manufacturing medicines, rubber and plastics, such as polythene. Lithium hydroxide is used to make lithium stearate, an ingredient in cosmetics and industrial greases used for cars, aircraft and ships. Lithium hydroxide has another important use, as a scrubber in submarines and spacecraft.

Scrubbers

Submarines cannot get fresh air under water nor can astronauts obtain fresh air in space. A scrubber is a device that recycles the air inside, keeping it fit for the crew to breathe. The simplest scrubbers contain solid lithium hydroxide, which **reacts** with carbon dioxide, removing it from the air as the crew respires.

The word equation for the reaction between lithium hydroxide and carbon dioxide is:

lithium hydroxide + carbon dioxide → lithium carbonate + water

---

Apollo 13

When Apollo 13 got into trouble on the way to the Moon in 1970, the crew had to squeeze into the lunar module for the journey back to Earth. To fit the square lithium hydroxide canisters from the command module into the round holes of the lunar module scrubbers, they used sticky tape, cardboard and plastic bags. If this hadn't worked, their own carbon dioxide would have killed them.

Some machines in submarines and spacecraft produce small amounts of acidic gases such as hydrogen chloride. These gases are absorbed by filters containing lithium carbonate.

The word equation for the reaction between lithium carbonate and hydrogen chloride is:

$$\text{lithium carbonate} + \text{hydrogen chloride} \rightarrow \text{lithium chloride} + \text{water} + \text{carbon dioxide}$$

Welding and air conditioners

Fluxes are substances that are used when metals are joined together by **welding**, brazing or soldering. Lithium fluoride is used in fluxes for joining metals such as copper, aluminium and magnesium. Concentrated solutions of lithium bromide or lithium chloride are used in the large air conditioning machines found in shops, hotels and hospitals. These liquids are part of the refrigeration equipment that chills the air.

▲
A foundry worker, wearing protective clothing and goggles, soldering copper. The bar of copper in his left hand is melted with a blow-torch and is used to join sheets of metal together. Fluxes containing lithium fluoride help to solder copper and other metals.

Lithium-ion batteries

Rechargeable lithium-**ion** batteries are used to power portable electronic equipment such as cell phones, laptop computers and video cameras. The negative electrodes in lithium-ion batteries are made from complex materials, such as lithium manganese oxide. They release electricity for a longer time than other types of battery of a similar size, such as nickel-cadmium (NiCad) batteries and produce 3.6V. Although they are more expensive, fewer batteries are needed so they can be more economical in some situations.

Sodium

A soft, silvery metal, sodium **reacts** rapidly with air and water. It is stored in oil to prevent this happening.

The discovery of sodium

People have known about sodium **compounds** and used them for thousands of years, but sodium itself was not discovered until 1807 because naturally it is always combined with other **elements**. Once Alessandro Volta invented the battery, chemists had the tool they needed to discover reactive metals like sodium. When Sir Humphry Davy used a battery to pass electricity through molten 'caustic soda', which we now know is sodium hydroxide, he discovered sodium metal forming at the negative electrode.

▲ *A block of sodium metal in a dish. It is usually stored in oil to stop it reacting with air and water.*

The name sodium comes from 'sodanum', the Roman name for a plant called glasswort that grows on salt marshes. Glasswort was used as a herbal medicine to cure headaches. It was burned to produce ashes that contained sodium carbonate and these were used in glass making. The symbol for sodium (Na) comes from 'natrium', the Roman name for sodium carbonate.

Volta's battery

An Italian scientist, called Alessandro Volta, invented the first battery in 1799, which is where the electrical term 'volts' comes from. His 'voltaic pile' was made from a stack of copper and zinc discs, each separated by a piece of cloth soaked in concentrated salt water. Chemists were keen to see what would happen to different chemicals when electricity was passed through them and they rushed to build their own batteries. Sir Humphry Davy was particularly successful with his battery, discovering sodium and potassium in 1807. A year later he became the first person to isolate magnesium, calcium, strontium and barium.

Sodium minerals

There are only five elements more plentiful than sodium in the Earth's crust. On average, each tonne of rock contains over twenty kilograms of sodium in various compounds. The most common is sodium chloride, found in rock salt or halite, but sodium is found in other minerals such as sodalite, cryolite and Chile saltpetre, also known as soda nitre.

Each cubic metre of seawater contains about twenty-six kilograms of sodium chloride. This means that the oceans contain a mind-boggling thirty-five thousand trillion tonnes. If you were around when the world began four and a half billion years ago and started measuring out a tonne of sea salt every four seconds, you would have only just finished!

▼ *Huge mounds of common salt, sodium chloride, at the Lake Grassmere salt works in New Zealand.*

Uses of sodium

About seventy thousand tonnes of sodium metal are produced in the world each year. It is **extracted** from rock salt or salt recovered from seawater by evaporation. Apart from being very **reactive**, sodium has other useful properties and some surprising uses.

Extraction of sodium

Sodium is extracted from sodium chloride using **electrolysis** in a container called a Downs Cell. The sodium chloride is first mixed with calcium chloride to lower the melting temperature to about 600 °C, saving energy and reducing costs. When electricity is passed through molten sodium chloride, it decomposes or breaks down to form sodium metal and chlorine gas.

Sodium and titanium

Sodium is used to extract titanium from its **ores** using the Kroll Process, invented by William Kroll in 1932. Titanium is a light but strong metal that does not rust. It is used in the aircraft industry and for the artificial joints used in joint replacement surgery. In the Kroll Process, liquid titanium chloride is heated with sodium or magnesium in an unreactive argon atmosphere. This forms titanium and sodium chloride. The sodium chloride is dissolved in water and washed away, leaving the titanium behind.

The word equation for the reaction between titanium chloride and sodium is:

titanium chloride + sodium → titanium + sodium chloride

The reaction happens because sodium is more reactive than titanium and displaces titanium from its **compounds**.

Sodium is used as the coolant in some designs of nuclear reactors. This 'Superphénix' reactor near Lyon in France contained four and a half thousand tonnes of sodium.

Sodium in nuclear reactors

Power stations use steam to drive turbines, which in turn drive the generators. Nuclear reactors use the heat produced from **nuclear reactions** to make steam. The heat must be carried out of the reactor by a 'coolant' so it can boil the water. Sodium is often used as a coolant in nuclear reactors because it has a high heat capacity, which means it can store a lot of heat. It also melts into a runny liquid at only 98 °C, so it can be pumped through tubes inside the reactor.

Nuclear reactors

*The fuel in nuclear reactors usually contains uranium. When a uranium **atom** splits in a nuclear reaction it fires off two or three high-speed **neutrons**. If these hit other uranium atoms, the atoms split and give off even more neutrons causing a chain reaction. A huge amount of heat is produced as well as neutrons and other **radiation**. Sodium slows down neutrons that whizz around inside the reactor, making them more likely to split uranium atoms.*

Sodium must not be allowed to cool down or it will solidify inside the tubes and pumps. It must not be permitted to leak into the air or water either because it will react with them and explode.

Sodium chloride

Sodium chloride is often called 'common salt' or just 'salt'. It is the most common sodium **compound** and over two hundred million tonnes of salt are produced each year.

Salt and salt deposits

Salt is a white solid that forms box-shaped crystals. It dissolves easily in water, each litre of seawater containing on average 26g. Salt reserves around the world are almost unlimited and underground deposits of rock salt are found in many places. The deposits were formed when water in ancient oceans evaporated.

Let them eat salt

Sodium is vital for our muscles, nerves and other cells to function properly and salt is the main source of sodium in our diet. A healthy diet easily provides adequate amounts of salt, as it is naturally present in food and often added as flavouring. Salt is also a food preservative, which acts by removing water, making it difficult for microorganisms to grow. However, eating too much salt can cause high blood pressure, which leads to heart problems. Grazing animals often need extra salt in their diet because the plants they eat do not provide enough sodium. Farmers provide salt blocks for their livestock to lick and may also mix salt into their food.

▲ *Crystals of common salt or sodium chloride, viewed through a microscope.*

Salt and salaries

Roman soldiers were paid partly with a ration of salt, called the 'salarium'. Later, a part of their wages was supposed to be for buying salt. We get the word salary from this.

Gritty roads

One of the major uses for salt is de-icing roads and paths in the winter. Salt lowers the melting point of ice so that it thaws, even when the temperature is below 0 °C. It is often mixed with a small amount of grit (crushed rock) to make it easier for tyres and shoes to get a good grip on the ground. Gritting the roads is a relatively cheap way to make roads safer in winter, although snowploughs are still necessary if snow is on the ground. The problem with using salt in winter is that it damages the steel reinforcing rods in roads and bridges and causes cars and other vehicles to rust more quickly. It also kills the plants on inland verges, but amazingly, seaside plants that can grow in salty conditions have colonized some inland roadsides.

◀ Rock salt is spread on icy roads in winter to melt the ice. This helps to keep the road clear and stops cars and other vehicles skidding.

The chlor-alkali industry

Although sodium chloride is used to flavour popcorn or fish and chips, it is also an important raw material for producing other chemicals. These include hydrogen, chlorine and an **alkali** called sodium hydroxide. Not surprisingly, the industry that produces these chemicals is called the chlor-alkali industry.

Electrolysis of brine

Brine is a very concentrated sodium chloride solution, usually produced by solution mining. When electricity is passed through brine, chlorine gas is formed at the positive electrode. You might expect sodium metal to be deposited at the negative electrode, but instead it **reacts** immediately with the water in the brine, forming hydrogen gas and a sodium hydroxide solution. It is quite easy to carry out this reaction in the laboratory, but it becomes more complicated on an industrial scale, especially as hydrogen and chlorine react together explosively!

Solution mining

Rock salt can be mined using cutting tools, but it is also **extracted** using a process called solution mining. Water is pumped down into the salt deposit and dissolves the salt to produce brine. Air is then pumped in, which pushes the brine to the surface through a pipe.

This diagram shows how solution mining works. Underground salt deposits can be over a kilometre deep. After the salt has been removed, old salt caverns may be used to store oil or industrial waste.

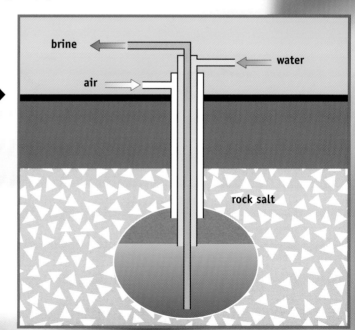

brine

water

air

rock salt

The mercury cell

Throughout the last century the mercury cell was used for the industrial **electrolysis** of brine. Sodium was prevented from dissolving in water and producing hydrogen at the same time as chlorine by using a layer of mercury as the negative electrode. The sodium dissolved in the mercury instead of the water to form a mixture of metals, called an amalgam. This was mixed with water later, well away from the chlorine gas. The sodium in the amalgam reacts with the water, producing sodium hydroxide solution and hydrogen gas. Smaller, more efficient devices are now replacing mercury cells.

The membrane cell

The membrane cell, developed in the 1970s, has a positive electrode made from titanium and a negative electrode made from nickel. The hydrogen and chlorine are kept apart by a special layer, called the membrane. The membrane cell uses less electricity than the mercury cell and it is kinder to the environment because it does not use poisonous mercury.

Chlorine and hydrogen

Sodium hydroxide is not the only useful chemical produced by the chlor-alkali industry. Chlorine is used in the manufacture of many products, including PVC plastic, paints, bleach and chemicals to kill bacteria in swimming pools. Hydrogen is used in the manufacture of margarine and nylon.

▲
Chlorine is one of the important chemicals produced by the chlor-alkali industry. It is used in the manufacture of many products, including chemicals that kill bacteria in swimming pools.

Sodium hydroxide and more

Forty-five million tonnes of sodium hydroxide or caustic soda, as it is known in industry, are produced each year by the **electrolysis** of brine. It is the cheapest **alkali** available and widely used in industry to **neutralize** acids such as the sulphuric acid used in oil **refining**. It is also an important material for the manufacture of many familiar substances.

Aluminium and soap

Sodium hydroxide is used to purify the aluminium oxide **extracted** from aluminium **ore**. Every tonne of purified aluminium oxide needs about 100kg of sodium hydroxide. Just like lithium hydroxide, sodium hydroxide will **react** with oils and fats to produce **compounds** such as sodium stearate, used in soap.

Liquid soaps, shampoos and shower gels contain sodium compounds such as sodium stearate and sodium laureth sulphate. These help to clean dirty skin and hair and make bubbles and foam.

Paper and artificial fibres

Paper is made from wood, but the wood must be processed to make wood pulp before it can be used. In the kraft process, wood chips are boiled with sodium hydroxide and sodium sulphite, Na_2SO_3. This produces a dark brown pulp that is used to make strong paper grocery bags and cardboard.

Rayon is the oldest synthetic commercial fibre. It is made using cellulose from wood pulp, which is turned into a thick, syrupy substance called viscose, using sodium hydroxide and carbon disulphide. The viscose is sprayed through fine holes into dilute sulphuric acid, which neutralizes the sodium hydroxide and turns the viscose into threads of rayon. Rayon has many uses including clothing, carpets and bandages. Cellophane wrapping film is also made from viscose.

Food and photography

Sodium sulphite and sodium metabisulphite, $Na_2S_2O_5$, are used in the food industry to preserve many foods including jam, dried fruit and drinks. In the beer and wine industries, sodium metabisulphite is used to sterilize the equipment before the ingredients are added.

◀ *Dried fruits are often treated with sodium sulphite or sodium metabisulphite, which stops them turning brown in the air.*

Sodium sulphite and sodium metabisulphite are used in photography to preserve the developing and fixing fluids. In addition, sodium metabisulphite is sometimes used in the stop bath, which halts the developing process. Sodium sulphite is used to manufacture sodium thiosulphate, $Na_2S_2O_3$, which is sometimes called 'hypo' and is commonly used as a fixer. It reacts with the silver compounds remaining in the film or photographic paper, stopping them turning dark and spoiling the photograph.

Sodium sulphate

Over six million tonnes of sodium sulphate, Na_2SO_4, are used around the world each year. It is found naturally as a **mineral** called mirabilite and is a by-product of rayon production and other processes. Sodium sulphate is used to recycle many of the chemicals involved in paper making. Nearly half of it is used as an inexpensive **filler** in washing powders that helps keep the powder dry until use.

Soda ash

Sodium carbonate, Na_2CO_3, is often called soda ash by the chemical industry. It is found in a **mineral** called trona and the world's biggest deposit is in Wyoming, USA. Alternatively, sodium carbonate can be made using the Solvay process. It is an important chemical and over thirty million tonnes of it are produced each year.

The Solvay process

*The Solvay process was invented in 1865 by a Belgian chemist called Ernest Solvay. There are several complex steps, one of which involves producing sodium hydrogencarbonate by **reacting** sodium chloride, carbon dioxide, ammonia and water. When the sodium hydrogencarbonate is heated, it breaks down to form sodium carbonate:*

$$\text{sodium hydrogen carbonate} \xrightarrow{\text{heat}} \text{sodium carbonate} + \text{carbon dioxide} + \text{water}$$

Glass making

To make glass, sand has to be melted. Sodium carbonate is added to reduce the melting temperature by half to 800 °C. Unfortunately, because the glass contains sodium carbonate it dissolves in water! To prevent this, calcium carbonate and magnesium carbonate are added to the glass while it is molten. Ordinary bottle glass or soda-lime glass is made in this way. Over 200kg of sodium carbonate are required to make each tonne of glass and half the sodium carbonate produced is used in this way.

Washing soda

Sodium carbonate is used in household cleaning products and can be bought as 'washing soda'. It produces an **alkaline** solution when dissolved in water. Sodium carbonate bleaches cotton and removes greasy stains but it also irritates skin, so wear rubber gloves if you use it!

Sodium hydrogencarbonate

Sodium hydrogencarbonate, $NaHCO_3$, is also called sodium bicarbonate or 'baking soda'. It dissolves in water to make a weak alkaline solution and produces carbon dioxide gas if heated or mixed with acids. Baking powder and self-raising flour contain sodium hydrogencarbonate and a dry acid such as tartaric acid. These react together when mixing a cake and the carbon dioxide produced helps the cake to rise when it is baked.

Our stomachs produce hydrochloric acid to help digest our food, but if it makes too much we get indigestion. A drink of water containing some sodium hydrogencarbonate helps by **neutralizing** these acids. Bacteria in the mouth produce acids that can damage teeth and some toothpastes contain sodium hydrogencarbonate, which work in the same way.

The word equation for the reaction between sodium hydrogencarbonate and hydrochloric acid is:

sodium hydrogencarbonate + hydrochloric acid → sodium chloride + water + carbon dioxide

One design of fire extinguisher uses the reaction between sodium hydrogencarbonate and sulphuric acid to produce carbon dioxide gas. This forces water out of the extinguisher and on to the flames.

◀ *Glass drinks bottles being made in a glass factory. Air is blown into molten glass in a mould to form the shape of the bottle.*

Potassium

Potassium is very similar to lithium and sodium, as it is a soft, silvery metal. Its **reaction** with air and water is rather lively, so it is also stored in oil.

The discovery of potassium

People have used potassium **compounds** for thousands of years, mainly for their **alkaline** properties, but it is never found as a pure metal because it is too reactive. It was not until 1807 that Sir Humphry Davy discovered potassium by passing electricity through molten 'caustic potash' or potassium hydroxide. To do this he used the battery invented by Alessandro Volta, just eight years earlier. Apparently he was so thrilled when he saw silvery potassium metal forming at the negative electrode and bursting into flames that he danced around his laboratory!

The symbol for potassium (K) comes from 'kalium', the Latin word for alkali. Potassium gets its name from 'potash' – the ashes from a pot! People used the ashes from burnt wood to make soap. They boiled the ashes in a pot with water, which released the alkalis from them. Then they boiled animal fats with the alkalis to make soap.

▼ *This digging machine is scraping minerals containing potassium compounds from the roof of a potash mine.*

Ashes and alkalis

People have made alkalis for thousands of years by boiling the ashes from plants in water. The word alkali comes from the Arabic words 'al-qali', which means 'the ash'.

Potassium minerals

Potassium is the seventh most abundant **element** in the Earth's crust. On average each tonne of rock contains about fifteen kilograms of potassium in various compounds, including sylvite and carnallite. These both contain potassium chloride. Seawater contains potassium chloride, as it does sodium chloride, but 28 times less. The word potash is often used to describe potassium oxide, but in the **minerals** industry this term is used for potassium minerals in general.

◀ *On average, each litre of seawater contains 10.7g of dissolved sodium and 0.38g of dissolved potassium. Seawater from Wormly in southern England is used as the international standard for seawater composition.*

Extraction of potassium

Unlike sodium, which can be produced from sodium chloride using **electrolysis**, potassium cannot be **extracted** from potassium chloride this way. This is because potassium chloride has a high melting point, which would make the process expensive and any potassium produced would just dissolve in the molten potassium chloride. Instead, potassium chloride is heated with sodium. Under normal circumstances there would not be a reaction because sodium is less reactive than potassium. However, the conditions are carefully adjusted so that a small amount of potassium vapour is produced, which is cooled and solidified.

Uses of potassium

Potassium metal itself has very few uses. At room temperature potassium and sodium are both solid, but a mixture of 78 per cent potassium and 22 per cent sodium is liquid. This unusual **alloy** is used as an industrial **catalyst** and as a cooling fluid in some nuclear reactors.

Radioactive potassium

Radioactive potassium is used as a 'tracer' in medicine. Tracers are chemicals injected into the body to help doctors diagnose illness. Doctors can study where radioactive tracers go by detecting the **radiation** they produce. Only tiny amounts are needed. Potassium-42 is a radioactive **isotope** used by doctors to find out how much potassium there is in a patient's bloodstream. It is also used to study the heart and the flow of blood through it. Potassium-42 **decays** or breaks down very quickly, to form an isotope of calcium that is not radioactive.

Isotopes

*All **atoms** of a particular **element** have the same number of **protons** and **electrons**, but different isotopes of an element have different numbers of **neutrons**. This gives them a different **mass number**. The most abundant or common isotope of potassium is potassium-39. Its **nucleus** contains nineteen protons and twenty neutrons. Potassium-42 has three more neutrons in its nucleus.*

Potassium-argon dating

The age of rocks can be calculated accurately, using a method called potassium-argon dating. Rocks usually contain potassium **compounds** and some of the potassium will be a radioactive isotope called potassium-40.

This is the fossil of a trilobite, a ▶ sea creature that lived about 380 million years ago. The age of the fossil can be worked out using potassium-argon dating.

Potassium-40 has a **half-life** of over a billion years, decaying very slowly to form argon-40. Geologists work out the age of a rock by comparing the amounts of these two isotopes. Young rocks have more potassium-40 than argon-40, and older rocks have more argon-40 than potassium-40.

Half-life

If we study lots of atoms, we cannot say when an individual atom will decay, but we can predict the time it takes for half of them to decay. This time is called its half-life. Potassium-39 does not seem to decay at all, whilst other isotopes, like potassium-40, decay very slowly. Potassium-49 decays extremely quickly, having a half-life of just one and a quarter seconds.

Potassium superoxide

Potassium metal is used to produce a yellow compound called potassium superoxide, KO_2. This is used in emergency breathing apparatus because it releases oxygen when it **reacts** with carbon dioxide or water. Bulky air cylinders are not needed and the apparatus can be put on quickly in an emergency.

◀ *This scuba diver is using a rebreather. This type of breathing apparatus converts used air into breathable air.*

The word equations for the reactions with potassium superoxide in the breathing apparatus are:

potassium superoxide + carbon dioxide → potassium carbonate + oxygen

potassium superoxide + water → potassium hydroxide + oxygen

Carbon dioxide and moisture in the breath are absorbed and converted into breathable oxygen.

Potassium compounds

Most potassium **compounds** will dissolve in water, like most sodium compounds, and can be used in all sorts of situations.

Drain cleaner and soap

Potassium hydroxide dissolves in water to produce a strongly **alkaline** solution, which can **react** with oils and fats. This makes it a very useful ingredient for drain cleaners. When drains become blocked, the blockage usually contains grease from household waste. The potassium hydroxide in the drain cleaner reacts with the grease, turning it into a soapy mixture that dissolves in water, helping to clear the drain.

Soap can be made by boiling potassium hydroxide solution with vegetable oils, such as palm oil. Different oils produce a variety of compounds, which can be blended together in different amounts to make a wide range of soaps. Potassium hydroxide is also used in the manufacture of potassium phosphate, an ingredient in liquid detergents and artificial **fertilizers**.

Fertilizers

Plants need **elements** such as nitrogen, phosphorus and potassium to grow properly. Potassium helps them produce healthy shoots and leaves, making them resistant to disease. If there is insufficient potassium in the soil, plants suffer from potassium deficiency. Abnormally short stems and leaves that curl and turn yellow are symptoms of this. Farmers add fertilizers to the soil to prevent this happening. These fertilizers contain compounds such as potassium sulphate and potassium chloride. Potassium nitrate is particularly useful as a fertilizer because it provides the plants with nitrogen as well as potassium.

Food and teeth

Potassium nitrate (with sodium nitrate) is used to preserve processed foods, such as bacon and sausages. It is also the active ingredient in most types of toothpaste used for sensitive teeth. Potassium nitrate is a powerful **oxidizing** agent used in matches and gunpowder.

Oxidizing agents

Many substances react slowly with the oxygen in air. However, if the temperature is high enough they may catch fire and burn. If we want something to burn really quickly or to burn in a situation where there is no air, like in space, we need to supply extra oxygen. Chemicals called oxidizing agents can supply extra oxygen and these include potassium nitrate, KNO_3.

Matches and fireworks

The potassium nitrate in a match head helps to light the match and enables the chemicals in gunpowder to burn quickly enough to cause an explosion. Potassium chlorate, $KClO_3$, is another powerful oxidizing agent used in matches and explosives, especially in fireworks.

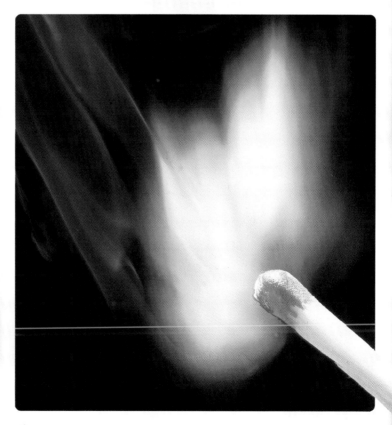

▲
Match heads contains potassium chlorate, phosphorus sulphide and powdered glass. When a match head is run across a rough surface, the heat from the friction causes it to burst into flames.

Potassium, sodium and our bodies

Potassium and sodium are both very important for cells in our bodies to work properly. They are needed to keep the different chemicals in our cells at the right concentration. Potassium **ions** are the most abundant metal ions inside cells, just as sodium ions are the most plentiful ions outside them. Cells even use energy to keep these two metals in balance.

The sodium-potassium pump

Cells use energy to move sodium out and potassium in. The energy comes from chemical bonds in a **compound** called adenosine triphosphate or ATP. The 'pump' is a protein in the cell membrane, which sticks to sodium and potassium ions and moves them in or out of the cell. For every **molecule** of ATP supplying energy to the pump, three sodium ions move out of the cell and two potassium ions move in.

Potassium and sodium in the diet

Potassium and sodium are needed for our nerves, heart and other muscles to function. A normal diet should provide enough potassium to keep us healthy. Foods that are rich in potassium include bananas, oranges, meat, potatoes and green vegetables. Salt is found in most foods, in fact some processed foods have salt added, to make them taste better. We are unlikely to suffer from sodium deficiency.

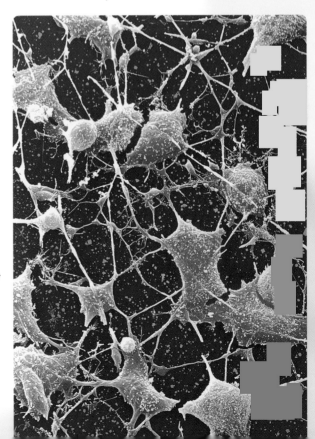

These are nerve cells viewed through an electron microscope. Information is passed between them using electrical nerve impulses, which need sodium and potassium ions to work. ▶

Low salt

Too much salt in our diet can lead to high blood pressure, which can cause heart disease and strokes. People suffering from high blood pressure are usually advised by their doctor to reduce their intake of salt. Choosing foods that contain less added salt can help and salt substitutes are available. These have two-thirds of the sodium chloride replaced with potassium chloride.

Rehydration salts

Patients who have lost a lot of body fluids may be given an intravenous 'drip' to replace the lost water and salt. This is a bag containing sterile sodium chloride solution, which is slowly added to the patient's bloodstream through a vein.

Tourists may suffer from diarrhoea on holiday and lose a lot of water as a result. They can also lose a lot of sodium and

potassium, which is dangerous if left untreated. In developing countries this can be fatal and over four million children a year died from untreated diarrhoea in the 1970s. By the start of this century, the death rate had been reduced by nearly three-quarters because of a simple mixture dissolved in water. The mixture is called oral rehydration salts or ORS for short. Treatment with ORS is really important in countries where there are few hospitals.

▲
A nurse preparing an intravenous drip containing sterile sodium chloride solution, which is added slowly through a vein into the patient's bloodstream to replace lost body fluids.

A recipe for ORS

sodium chloride	2.6g
potassium chloride	1.5g
sodium citrate	2.9g
glucose	13.5g
water	1 litre

Rubidium

Rubidium is a soft, silvery metal that **reacts** so quickly with air and water that it must be stored in unreactive argon gas. Rubidium melts at 39 °C and may become liquid on an extemely hot day.

The discovery of rubidium

Rubidium was discovered in 1861 by two German chemists, Gustav Kirchhoff and Robert Bunsen, whilst using a **spectroscope** to study the light emitted by the **mineral** lepidolite in a flame test. They named the new **element** rubidium, after the Latin word for dark red because its **spectrum** contains two dark red lines.

Extraction of rubidium

Rubidium is the sixteenth most abundant element in the Earth's crust although each tonne of rock only contains about sixty grams. Small amounts of it occur in various minerals, including pollucite, carnallite and lepidolite. Rubidium is usually obtained from the materials left over after the **extraction** of lithium from lepidolite. Several complex steps are needed to separate rubidium from the other elements in the waste material, which makes rubidium a relatively expensive metal.

Uses of rubidium

Rubidium is not only expensive, it is also difficult to handle safely because of its reactivity. Even some of its **compounds** can be hazardous. Rubidium is used as a 'getter' in some vacuum tubes. These electronic devices are now only used in expensive hi-fi systems, professional guitar amplifiers and the radio transmitters used by radio stations to broadcast their programmes. They were more widely used before the transistor was invented in 1947 and semi-conductors took over. To make a **vacuum** inside the vacuum tube, most of the air is removed from it at the factory using a pump. Then a small amount of reactive metal is put inside each tube before it is sealed. The metal is called a getter because it 'gets' any remaining air by reacting with it, producing a really good vacuum.

Rubidium is used in some designs of photoelectric cell. When light shines on them, a small electric current is produced, which stops if the light is removed. Rubidium can be made to give off **electrons** when light hits it, so it is used in the negative electrode of these devices. Photoelectric cells are used in all sorts of situations where a beam of light falling on them could be blocked. These include automatic doors in lifts and devices that count objects moving along conveyor belts in factories.

▼ *Vacuum tubes are electronic devices used in radio transmitters, some hi-fi systems and guitar amplifiers. Rubidium is one of the reactive metals used to remove traces of air from inside vacuum tubes.*

Caesium

Caesium is a very soft metal with a faint gold colour. It **reacts** so quickly with air and water that it must be stored in a **vacuum** or argon gas. Caesium melts at 28 °C and may turn into a very runny liquid if you hold its container.

The discovery of caesium

Gustav Kirchhoff and Robert Bunsen (below) discovered caesium in 1860, a year before they discovered rubidium. Caesium was named after the Latin word for sky blue because its **spectrum** contains two blue lines.

Robert Wilhelm Bunsen (1811–1899). Working with Gustav Kirchhoff, he examined the spectrum of light given off by the Sun and was able to identify the **elements** *in the Sun. They discovered caesium in 1860 and rubidium in 1861.*

Extraction of caesium

Caesium is quite rare in the Earth's crust and on average each tonne of rock contains just two grams of it. Like the other alkali metals, caesium never occurs naturally as a pure metal. Pollucite (caesium aluminium silicate) is a good source of caesium. It is also found in small amounts in other **minerals**, such as lepidolite, and can be **extracted** from the materials left over from lithium production. Several complex steps are needed to isolate caesium from other elements, especially rubidium, which is very similar chemically. One method involves purifying the caesium **compounds** and converting them into caesium cyanide. This is melted and broken down to form caesium by passing electricity through it.

Into space with caesium

Caesium is used as a 'getter' in vacuum tubes, just like rubidium. However, in the twentieth century it was involved in something far more exciting – developing engines for spacecraft.

Engines called **ion** drives are often mentioned in science fiction films, but these exist now. In an ordinary rocket engine, burning fuel produces hot gases that shoot out of the end of the rocket. These push the spacecraft into space and on to other planets. Ion engines work differently and are smaller and more efficient. High-speed **electrons** bombard the **atoms** in the fuel and cause them to lose some of their own electrons. The atoms become positively charged particles called ions and a powerful electric field accelerates them to about 40 km/s. The ions shoot out of the back of the engine and push the spacecraft forward. Unlike ordinary rockets, ion drives remain with the spacecraft for a long time, gradually accelerating the spacecraft to great speeds.

The first ion engines used caesium for their fuel. In 1974, a caesium ion engine was successfully tested on a satellite in space. Unfortunately, during the engine's ground tests tiny amounts of reactive caesium were sprayed everywhere. This was very messy and ion engines now use unreactive xenon gas as a fuel.

Atomic clocks

The best atomic clocks rely on caesium **atoms**, which are accurate to about one second in every twenty million years and ensure that clocks all over the world keep in step with each other. Many countries keep their own atomic clocks in national laboratories. They provide accurate time signals, which are important for computer networks like the Internet to work properly. All sorts of business rely on the signals to run smoothly, including television and radio stations, telephone and electric power companies.

The second

The second is the basic unit of time. As caesium clocks are so accurate, scientists define the second as the amount of time it takes for a caesium-133 atom to do exactly 9,192,631,770 vibrations.

Resonating caesium atoms

When you first learned how to use a swing, it is more than likely that you moved your legs too slowly or too quickly, you used a lot of energy and the swing hardly moved. However once your legs moved at the right speed you probably found that you could swing much higher. This is because more of your energy went into the swing. This is called the resonance frequency. Atoms do not play on swings, but they do have a resonance frequency.

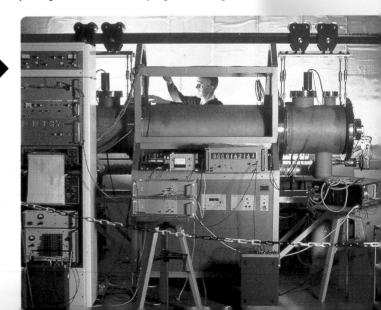

The CS$_2$ caesium atomic clock at the German National Standards Laboratory, near Hannover. Atomic clocks may not look like ordinary clocks or work like them, but they are incredibly accurate – usually to within at least one second in a million years.

In a caesium atomic clock, caesium is heated to boil off some atoms. These are exposed to microwaves and they vibrate as a result. The resonance frequency of caesium atoms is 9,192,631,770 vibrations per second, which can be measured very accurately. Electronic devices in the clock lock on to the resonance frequency, rather like tuning into a favourite radio station and the signals given off are used to measure time.

Radioactive caesium

When **radiation** is not controlled it damages healthy cells, causing cancer and other illnesses. However, managed **radioactivity** is an effective treatment for some cancers and radioactive caesium may be used in machines for this purpose.

Radiotherapy

A 'teletherapy' machine contains a radioactive **isotope** such as caesium-137. Caesium-137, which does not occur naturally, is radioactive and has a **half-life** of thirty years. A beam of radiation from the teletherapy machine is aimed at the cancerous growth, damaging and killing the cells. This treats some cancers very successfully.

The Goiânia accident

Goiânia is a city 180km southwest of the Brazilian capital, Brasília. In 1987, hundreds of people in Goiânia were accidentally exposed to radiation from caesium chloride that contained radioactive caesium-137. Men looking for scrap metal to sell broke into an old hospital and took apart an abandoned teletherapy machine. They found a white powder inside that sparkled and glowed blue in the dark. This was radioactive caesium chloride. It was passed around friends and relatives to look at, but no one realized how dangerous this was until people began to fall ill. Four people, including a child, eventually died and some contaminated houses had to be demolished. Brazil has changed the regulations that concern the disposal of radioactive materials to avoid anything like this happening again.

Caesium compounds

Caesium hydroxide is the strongest known **alkali** and will even **react** with glass. However it is used as a **catalyst** for some chemical reactions. Other caesium **compounds** are far less reactive, such as caesium chloride, which biochemists use to separate pieces of **DNA** with the help of a centrifuge.

Caesium azide

It is difficult to handle caesium safely because it melts easily and is very reactive. Caesium is often supplied as a compound of caesium and nitrogen, called caesium azide, CsN_3. This is a colourless solid that breaks down when heated to form caesium and nitrogen gas.

Centrifuges and caesium chloride

If water and sand grains are mixed together in a test tube, gravity pulls the sand to the bottom quickly. If powdered sand is used instead, it sinks very slowly because the particles are so small. Centrifuges help small particles like cells sink quickly. The test tubes are spun round and round at high speed and the particles are flung to the bottom very rapidly.

▼ *Centrifuges are used to separate the different components of blood and other substances. Plastic or glass tubes are loaded on to a rotor inside the centrifuge and then spun around very quickly.*

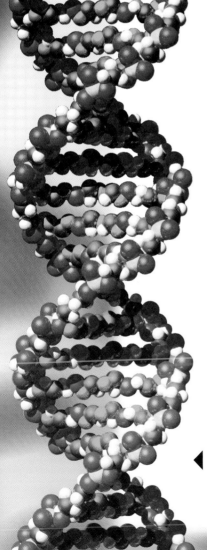

Solutions of caesium chloride are very **dense**. When spun in an ultracentrifuge, the caesium in the caesium chloride is pulled towards the bottom of the test tube. This makes the solution very dense at the bottom and less dense at the top.

DNA (deoxyribonucleic acid) is a long complex chemical, which carries the genetic information in cells. Biochemists often need to separate pieces of DNA for their research. Fortunately the DNA pieces all have different densities, which allows them to be separated using a centrifuge. Once in the ultracentrifuge, the DNA pieces are pulled towards the bottom of the test tube until each one reaches a part of the caesium chloride solution that has a matching density, where it remains. Layers of DNA are formed that are easily removed when the ultracentrifuge stops.

Infrared spectrometers
Crystals of caesium bromide or caesium iodide are used to make the 'windows' in infrared spectrometers because they are very good at letting infrared light pass through them. Chemists use these machines to analyze samples of their chemicals. Each chemical absorbs infrared light differently. The spectrometer measures how a beam of infrared light is changed as it passes through a sample and every chemical has a unique 'fingerprint' of results.

A model of a section of DNA or deoxyribonucleic acid, showing the famous 'double helix' spiral structure discovered by James Watson, Francis Crick and Rosalind Franklin in 1953.

Francium

Francium is an extremely rare, **radioactive** metal that no one has seen enough of to know what it looks like. Chemists can use the **periodic table** to predict its properties. It is likely to be extremely **reactive**, as **elements** in **group** 1 become more reactive going down the group and francium is at the bottom of the group. It would probably explode into flames if it came in contact with air and water and would need to be stored in a **vacuum**.

The discovery of francium

When Dimitri Mendeleev developed his periodic table, he realized not all the elements had been discovered. Mendeleev bravely left gaps in his table, ready to fit in the missing elements. This allowed chemists to predict the likely properties of the missing elements by studying those positioned around the gaps. It also gave them strong hints about which **minerals** might contain the missing elements. One of the gaps was for 'eka-caesium', which he expected would be located immediately below caesium. Francium, the missing eka-caesium, was discovered in 1939 by the French chemist, Marguerite Perey, who named the new element after her native country.

Marguerite Perey (1909–1975), who discovered francium while working as a technician at the Curie Institute in Paris. She later became the first woman member of the French Academy of Sciences.

Production of francium

Francium is very radioactive. It is formed when actinium, present in uranium **ores**, gives off **radiation**. Francium-223, its most abundant **isotope**, has a **half-life** of only twenty-two minutes and **decays** to form astatine and radium. This means that if you could manage to get a gram of it, after four hours there would be less than half a milligram left! This is why there are probably only a few grams of francium in the whole of the Earth's crust at any one time.

Modern alchemy

*The ancient alchemists tried in vain to convert lead into gold. They failed because in fact you need a **nuclear reaction** to convert one element into another – chemical reaction just cannot do it. To get a new artificial element with a bigger nucleus a machine called a particle accelerator is used to accelerate **ions** to tremendously high speeds. These are fired into a metal target and if the scientists are lucky, an atom and an ion stick together to make a new **atom** with a much larger **nucleus**.*

Francium has no uses, apart from scientific research. Scientists even have to make their own francium using nuclear reactions if they want to study it. One way to do this is to bombard gold with oxygen ions in a machine called a particle accelerator.

▼ *The inside of Linac, a particle accelerator at the Fermi National Accelerator Laboratory (Fermilab) near Chicago in the USA. Powerful electric fields accelerate particles such as **protons** to very high speeds.*

Find out more about the alkali metals

Some useful information about the alkali metals

Element	Symbol	Atomic number	Melting point (°C)	Boiling point (°C)	State at 25°C	Density at 25°C (g/cm^3)
lithium	Li	3	181	1327	solid	0.53
sodium	Na	11	98	883	solid	0.97
potassium	K	19	64	757	solid	0.86
rubidium	Rb	37	39	688	solid	1.53
caesium	Cs	55	28	678	solid	1.87
francium	Fr	87	not known	not known	probably solid	not known

Compounds

These tables show you the chemical formulae of most of the **compounds** mentioned in this book. For example, sodium sulphate has the formula Na_2SO_4. This means it is made from two sodium **atoms**, one sulphur atom and four oxygen atoms, joined together by chemical **bonds**.

Lithium compounds

Lithium compounds	formula
amblygonite	$LiAlFPO_4$
lepidolite	$KLi_2AlSi_4O_{10}(OH)F$
petalite	$LiAlSi_4O_{10}$
spodumene	$LiAlSi_2O_6$
lithium bromide	$LiBr$
lithium carbonate	Li_2CO_3
lithium chloride	$LiCl$
lithium fluoride	LiF
lithium hydroxide	$LiOH$
lithium oxide	Li_2O
lithium sulphate	Li_2SO_4

Sodium compounds	formula
cryolite	Na_3AlF_6
halite	$NaCl$
soda nitre	$NaNO_3$
sodalite	$Na_8Al_6Si_6O_{24}Cl_2$
trona	$Na_3(HCO_3)(CO_3)$
sodium carbonate	Na_2CO_3
sodium chloride	$NaCl$
sodium citrate	$Na_3C_6H_5O_7$
sodium hydrogencarbonate	$NaHCO_3$
sodium hydroxide	$NaOH$
sodium metabisulphite	$Na_2S_2O_5$
sodium stearate	$C_{17}H_{35}COONa$
sodium sulphate	Na_2SO_4
sodium sulphite	Na_2SO_3
sodium thiosulphate	$Na_2S_2O_3$

Potassium compounds	formula
carnallite	$KCl.MgCl_2$
sylvite	KCl
potassium carbonate	K_2CO_3
potassium chlorate	$KClO_3$
potassium chloride	KCl
potassium hydroxide	KOH
potassium nitrate	KNO_3
potassium oxide	K_2O
potassium sulphate	K_2SO_4
potassium superoxide	KO_2

Rubidium compounds	formula
rubidium superoxide	RbO_2

Find out more continued

Caesium compounds

Caesium compounds	formula
pollucite	$(CsNa)_2Al_2Si_4O_{12}$
caesium azide	CsN_3
caesium bromide	$CsBr$
caesium chloride	$CsCl$
caesium cyanide	$CsCN$
caesium hydroxide	$CsOH$
caesium iodide	CsI
caesium superoxide	CsO_2

Acids

Acid compounds	formula
hydrochloric acid	HCl
nitric acid	HNO_3
sulphuric acid	H_2SO_4

Other compounds

Other compounds	formula
ammonia	NH_3
calcium carbonate	$CaCO_3$
carbon dioxide	CO_2
carbon disulphide	CS_2
hydrogen chloride	HCl
magnesium carbonate	$MgCO_3$
tartaric acid	$C_4H_6O_6$
titanium chloride	$TiCl_4$
water	H_2O

Glossary

alloy mixture of two or more metals or mixture of a metal and a non-metal. Alloys are often more useful than the pure metal on its own.

alkali substance that will neutralize acids to form a salt and water. Alkalis are bases that dissolve in water.

atom smallest particle of an element that has the properties of that element. Atoms contain smaller particles called subatomic particles.

atomic number number of protons in the nucleus of an atom. It is also called the proton number. No two elements have the same atomic number.

bond force that joins atoms together

catalyst substance that speeds up reactions without getting used up

compound substance made from the atoms of two or more elements, joined together by chemical bonds. Compounds can be broken down into simpler substances, which may have different properties from the elements in them. For example, water is a liquid at room temperature, but it is made from two gases, hydrogen and oxygen.

decay when the nucleus of a radioactive substance breaks up, gives off radiation and becomes the nucleus of another element, it decays

density mass of a substance compared to its volume. To calculate the density of a substance, you divide its mass by its volume. Substances with a high density feel very heavy for their size.

DNA (deoxyribonucleic acid) long, complex chemical, which carries the genetic information and is the substance of inheritance for almost all living things

electrolysis breaking down or decomposing a compound by passing electricity through it. The compound must be molten or dissolved in a liquid for electrolysis to work.

electron subatomic particle with a negative electric charge. Electrons are found around the nucleus of an atom.

element substance made from one type of atom. Elements cannot be broken down into simpler substances. All substances are made from one or more elements.

extract remove a chemical from a mixture of chemicals

fertilizer chemical that gives plants the elements they need for healthy growth

filler substance added to a product to improve its properties

group vertical column of elements in the periodic table. Elements in a group have similar properties.

half-life time taken for half the atoms of a radioactive substance to decay

ion charged particle made when atoms lose or gain electrons. If a metal atom loses electrons it becomes a positive ion. If a non-metal atom gains electrons it becomes a negative ion.

isotope atom of an element with the same number of protons and electrons, but a different number of neutrons. Different isotopes share the same atomic number, but they have a different mass number.

mass number number of protons added to the number of neutrons, in the nucleus of an atom

mineral substance that is found naturally but does not come from animals or plants. Metal ores and limestone are examples of minerals.

molecule smallest unit of an element or compound that exists by itself. A molecule is usually made from two or more atoms joined together.

neutralize when an acid and an alkali or base react together. The resulting solution is neutral, which means it is not acidic or alkaline.

neutron subatomic particle with no electric charge. Neutrons are found in the nucleus of an atom.

nuclear reaction reaction involving the nucleus of an atom. Radiation is produced in nuclear reactions.

nucleus part of an atom made from protons and neutrons. It has a positive electric charge and is found at the centre of the atom.

ore mineral from which metals can be taken out and purified

oxidizing agent chemical that supplies or adds oxygen to other chemicals. These are also called oxidants.

period horizontal row of elements in the periodic table

periodic table table in which all the known elements are arranged into groups and periods

prism block of transparent material, usually glass, which has a triangular cross-section

proton subatomic particle with a positive electric charge. Protons are found in the nucleus of an atom.

radiation energy or particles given off when an atom decays

radioactive describes a substance that can produce radiation

reaction chemical change that produces new substances

refining removing impurities from a substance to make it more pure. It can also mean separating the different substances in a mixture, for example, in oil refining.

spectroscope piece of equipment that splits the light given off by something, into its spectrum

spectrum range of colours that make up a ray of light. The various colours of light have different spectra.

subatomic particle particle smaller than an atom, such as a proton, neutron or an electron

vacuum empty space containing very little air or none at all

welding joining two or more metals together, usually by heating them

Timeline

potassium discovered	1807	Sir Humphry Davy
sodium discovered	1807	Sir Humphry Davy
lithium discovered	1817	Johann Arfvedsen
caesium discovered	1860	Gustav Kirchhoff and Robert Bunsen
rubidium discovered	1861	Gustav Kirchhoff and Robert Bunsen
francium discovered	1939	Marguerite Perey

Further reading and useful websites

Books

Knapp, Brian, *The elements series*, particularly, *Sodium and Potassium* (Atlantic Europe Publishing Co., 1996)

Oxlade, Chris, *Chemicals in Action series*, particularly, *Acids and Bases* (Heinemann Library, 2002)

Oxlade, Chris, *Chemicals in Action series*, particularly, *Metals* (Heinemann Library, 2002)

Websites

WebElements™
http://www.webelements.com
An interactive periodic table crammed with information and photographs.

Proton Don
http://www.funbrain.com/periodic
The fun periodic table quiz!

Mineralogy Database
http://www.webmineral.com
Useful information about minerals, including colour photographs and information about their chemistry.

DiscoverySchool
http://school.discovery.com/clipart
Help for science projects and homework, and free science clip art.

BBC Science
http://www.bbc.co.uk/science
Quizzes, news, information and games about all areas of science.

Creative Chemistry
http://www.creative-chemistry.org.uk
An interactive chemistry site with fun practical activities, quizzes, puzzles and more.

Index

Titles in the *Periodic Table* series include:

Hardback   0 431 16995 0

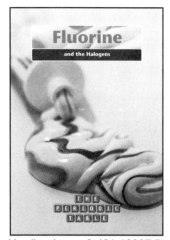

Hardback   0 431 16997 7

Hardback   0 431 16998 5

Hardback   0 431 16996 9

Hardback   0 431 16994 2

Hardback   0 431 16999 3

Find out about the other titles in this series on our website www.heinemann.co.uk/library